MEGA BOOKS
ANIMALS

NINA FILIPEK
AND SOPHIE GILES

Gareth Stevens
PUBLISHING

BE A SUPER SPOTTER

Study these pictures and look out for them as you read this book. Can you answer the super spotter questions?

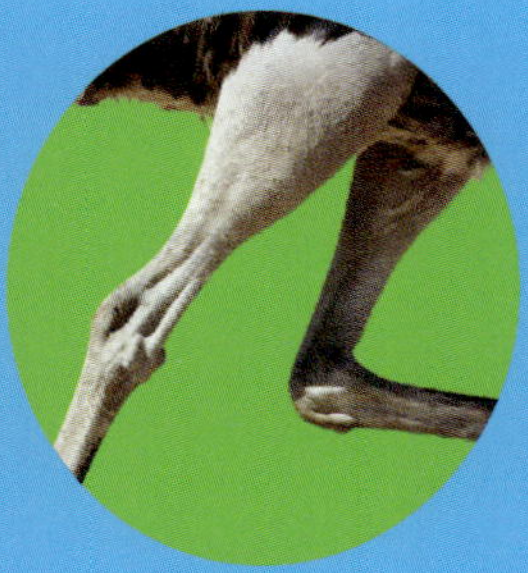

Whose legs are these?

Whose skin is this?

Whose tongue is this?

Whose beak is this?

Please visit our website, www.garethstevens.com. For a free color catalog of all our high-quality books, call toll free 1-800-542-2595 or fax 1-877-542-2596.

Published in 2025 by
Gareth Stevens Publishing
2544 Clinton St.
Buffalo, NY 14224

Written by: Nina Filipek and Sophie Giles

Images: Shutterstock.com (Heiko Kiera, E. O., PHOTOCREO Michal Bednarek, Nobby Clarke, Christian Musat, Eric Isselee, fivespots, Four Oaks, Simon Greig, Gelpi, ILYA AKINSHIN, Talvi, Gerrit_de_Vries, Daxiao Productions, Stu Porter, ESB Professional, Daniel Rose, axily, jaroslava V, Denise Thompson, Rosa Jay, Smileus, paula french, Christian Weber, Roman Samokhin, Oligo, Michael Shake, Svetlana Foote, Butterfly Hunter, Valentyna Chukhlyebova, Rawpixel.com, Attila JANDI, ixpert, chakkrachai nicharat, KitThanit, Roger Clark ARPS BPE, R.M. Nunes, Gallinago_media, Atomic Roderick, Catchlight Lens, Sriram Bird Photographer, Mojijung , dan_nurgitz, Lucie Galdova, un.bolovan, beltsazar, Anna Kucherova, megscapturedtreasures, Keneva Photography, Baishev, De Jongh Photography, wildestanimal, Allen Haggerty, Richard Fitzer, Zoe Ezzy, matthieu Gallet, Gary E Swanson, Phatthanit, ThomasLENNE, Milan Zygmunt, novama)

Cataloging-in-Publication Data

Names: Filipek, Nina. | Giles, Sophie.
Title: Animals / by Nina Filipek and Sophie Giles.
Description: Buffalo, NY : Gareth Stevens Publishing, 2025. | Series: Mega books
Identifiers: ISBN 9781482467871 (pbk.) | ISBN 9781482467888 (library bound) | ISBN 9781482467895 (ebook)
Subjects: LCSH: Animals--Juvenile literature.
Classification: LCC QL49.F51 F47 2025 | DDC 590--dc23

Printed in the United States of America

CPSIA compliance information: Batch #CSGS25: For further information contact Gareth Stevens at 1-800-542-2595.

CONTENTS

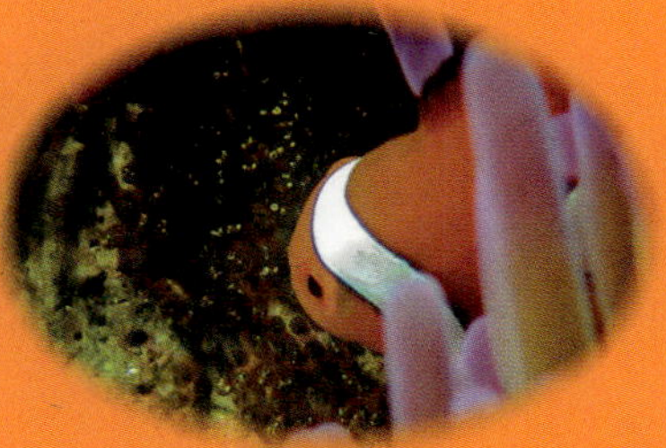

MEGA ANIMALS

Animals come in all shapes and sizes and have incredible abilities. They can be big like the elephant, tall like the giraffe, or fast like the cheetah. Some are fierce like the grizzly bear or venomous like a snake. Even a small insect, such as a dung beetle, can still be very strong!

Grizzly bear - one of the biggest bears and part of the brown bear family

Tallest animal - the giraffe

King cobra - the longest venomous snake

Fish are some of Earth's oldest animals

Fins, fur and feathers

Some animals have fur or hair to keep them warm. Others have feathers for flying or scales and fins for swimming. Many have special features, such as the color-changing chameleon. We'll meet all of these kinds of animals in this book.

Clever colors

Some animals have markings that help them hide or blend into the background. This is called camouflage. Others stand out from the crowd, like this brightly colored scarlet macaw.

The scarlet macaw's colorful feathers help it to attract a mate.

Largest animal on land – the African elephant

A chameleon's colors can even change to match what it feels!

Fastest animal on land – the cheetah

The tiny dung beetle is the strongest animal for its body weight. It can pull 1,140 times its own weight!

MASSIVE MAMMALS

The blue whale is the largest animal that has ever lived. It is as long as three buses, and its tongue weighs as much as a rhinoceros. Even more amazingly, it grows to this massive size by eating tiny sea creatures called krill. In one day, a blue whale eats more krill than two adult giraffes weigh!

Huge mouth filters krill from the water

Blue whale

The blue whale's call is as loud as a volcano erupting or a rocket launching.

Biggest on land

The African elephant is the biggest animal living on land. It can weigh as much as four cars, and grow to be up to 13 feet (4 m) tall! It is a herbivore (a plant eater) and eats enormous amounts of grass, fruit, roots, tree bark, and twigs to feed its big appetite.

Can you point to?

a tusk

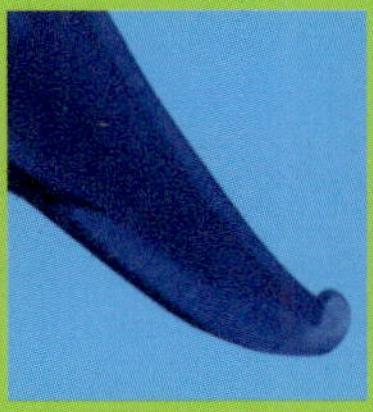
a flipper

a nostril

What does the blue whale eat?

An animal this big can only live in the ocean, where the water supports its weight!

Weighs as much as 16 double-decker buses

Up to 100 feet (30 m) in length

Second-largest

The white rhinoceros is the second-largest land animal by weight. Its large horns make it look fierce, but, like elephants, rhinos only eat plants!

The rhinoceros has an excellent sense of smell and hearing, but its eyesight is poor.

ARMORED ANIMALS

The giant tortoise has a hard shell that protects its body. When it feels threatened, it tucks its head and legs into its shell and hides. These tortoises are known for their long lives. Some have lived as long as 200 years, and some scientists think they might live for up to 500 years!

Up close

Here you can see the giant tortoise's eyes and nostrils. It doesn't have teeth. Instead, this herbivore has a "beak" that it uses like teeth to bite off cactus leaves, fruits, vines, and other vegetation to eat.

A giant tortoise can weigh as much as four people!

Can you point to?

scaly skin

quills

claws

Armored armadillo

This strange-looking animal is an armadillo. It has thick skin, like a suit of armor. When in danger, it can tuck its soft snout and legs inside its hard coat and roll into a ball.

Armadillos mostly eat beetles, ants, and termites, which they dig up from the ground.

How does a tortoise use its shell?

Can grow to be 5 feet (1.5 m) tall!

Super spiky

This Indian crested porcupine has spiky hairs on its head and back for protection. These hairs, called quills, are hard and very sharp.

TALLEST AND LONGEST

The giraffe is the tallest of the land animals. It is so tall (up to 20 feet [6 m]) that it can eat the leaves from the tops of trees. Being tall also means it can spot lions from far away. Lions are its main predator. They hunt giraffes for food.

Big babies

When they are born, calves (baby giraffes) are up to 6 feet (1.8 m) tall. That's as tall as some adult humans!

Look how tall the baby giraffe is compared to this boy!

Which animal hunts giraffes?

Legs are almost 6.5 feet (2 m) long

Hair-covered horns called ossicones

Giraffe

Giraffes have the same number of bones in their necks as humans!

The giraffe's markings give it camouflage. No two giraffes have the same markings.

Giraffes have long tongues to reach the highest leaves!

Can you point to?

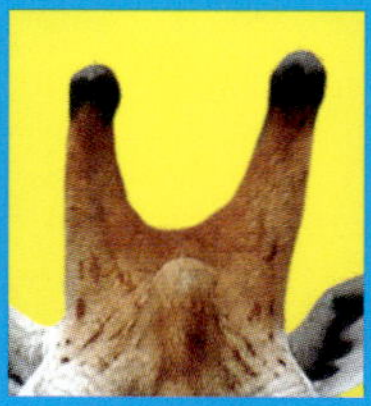

two horns

an ear

a tail

What is a predator?

Animals that hunt and eat other animals are called predators.

Longest snakes

Some phythons can grow to over 26 feet (8 m) long. That's longer than four adult humans lying head to foot! They have four rows of teeth in their upper jaw and two rows in their lower jaw. They can open their jaws wide enough to swallow a sheep, pig, monkey, or deer whole!

Speedy sprinter

When escaping from predators, giraffes can run fast (up to 37 miles [60 km] per hour) over a short distance.

Reticulated python

BIG CATS

A male lion is often called the "king of the jungle," perhaps because their manes look like crowns. But lions don't live in jungles. They live on rocky hills and grassy savannas. A big, dark mane shows that a male lion is fit and healthy, and helps it to attract a mate, somewhat like the long, colorful tail feathers of the peacock.

Why do male lions have manes?

Disappearing spots

Lion cubs have spots on their fur to camouflage them and keep them safe. These markings fade as the cubs grow and no longer need the protection of the camouflage.

Lion

Tiger

The tiger is the biggest wild cat. They can eat up to 100 pounds (45 kg) of meat in one meal (the weight of an average 13-year-old child!) but then not eat again for many days. They often hunt at night, near waterholes where their prey comes to drink.

A tiger's stripes help it blend in with its surroundings.

Lion's pride

Lions live in a family group called a pride. A large number of lionesses (female lions), cubs, and a few young males make up a pride.

FASTEST ON LAND

For many animals, speed is essential for survival. Predators need to be fast to catch their food, and their prey needs to be fast to escape being eaten! The fastest land animals have long, strong legs and lightweight bodies.

Can you point to?

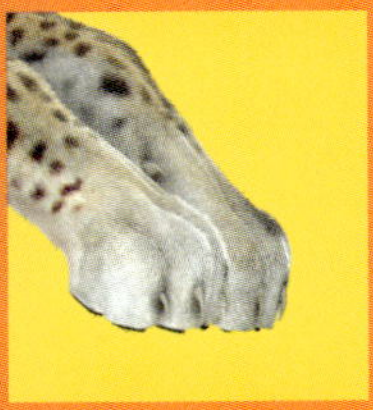
a paw

spotted fur

a curvy neck

What do cheetahs eat?

Fast cat

The cheetah is the world's fastest animal on land. It can sprint at speeds of up to 75 miles (120 km) per hour when chasing a meal, such as a gazelle or an impala. That's as fast as some cars driving along a highway!

Lion family

In the lion family, the females do most of the hunting because they are the fastest runners. The male lions are bigger, heavier, and slower.

Lionesses (female lions) are leaner and lighter than males.

Excellent eyesight

At top speed, a cheetah's stride is over 23 feet (7 m) long.

Cheetah

What is prey?

Animals that are hunted and eaten by other animals are called prey.

Fastest on two legs

The ostrich is the largest bird on Earth. It can't fly, but it can run up to almost 45 miles (70 km) per hour over a short distance when chased by predators, such as lions.

Ostriches use their wings to help them balance when changing direction at high speed.

AWESOME REPTILES

The crocodile is one of the oldest creatures on Earth. It is as old as the dinosaurs. A crocodile's jaws are 50 times stronger than a human's. It has between 60 and 72 teeth at a time and as many as 8,000 teeth in its lifetime. Like sharks, as one tooth falls out, another takes its place.

Why are a crocodile's eyes on the top of its head?

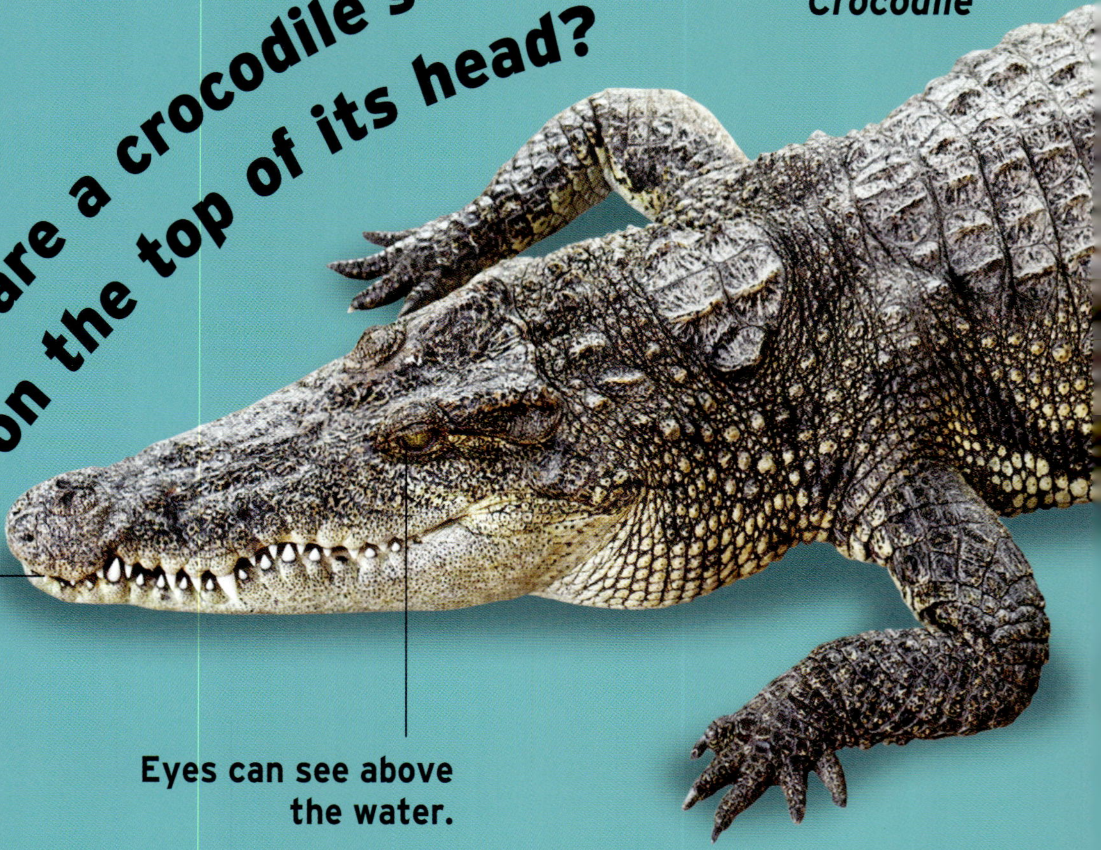

They eat anything!

Alligators and crocodiles will eat anything they can catch: fish, frogs, and turtles. Crocodiles even attack buffalo! They don't chew their food. Instead, they rip, tear, and crush it, then swallow it in large chunks.

Deadly dragon

The Komodo dragon is the largest lizard on Earth. Even big animals such as buffalo cannot survive its deadly bite. Venom glands release venom into the wound. This weakens its prey, and allows the dragon to follow and kill the animal later if it doesn't die immediately.

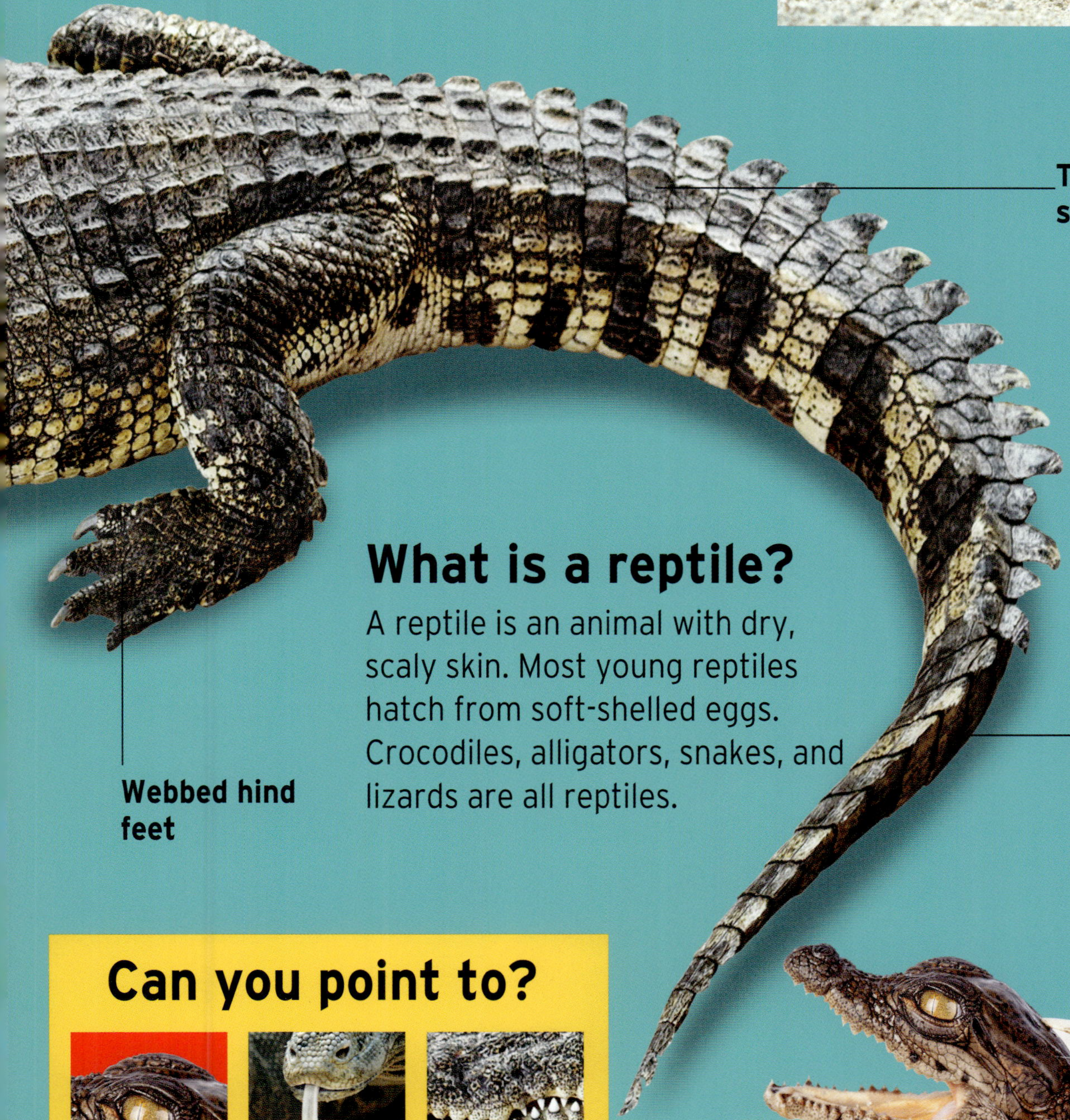

What is a reptile?

A reptile is an animal with dry, scaly skin. Most young reptiles hatch from soft-shelled eggs. Crocodiles, alligators, snakes, and lizards are all reptiles.

Baby crocodile hatching

Can you point to?

an eye

a tongue

teeth

AMAZING APES

Chimpanzees are some of the cleverest animals. They have learned how to use tools, such as sticks to "fish" for termites, rocks to crack open nuts, and leaves to soak up water to drink. In many ways they are like us: they can walk tall on their back legs and can laugh, show sadness, and feel happy.

Chimpanzee

Chimps groom each other's hair.

A closed mouth shows a chimp is not aggressive.

Can you point to?

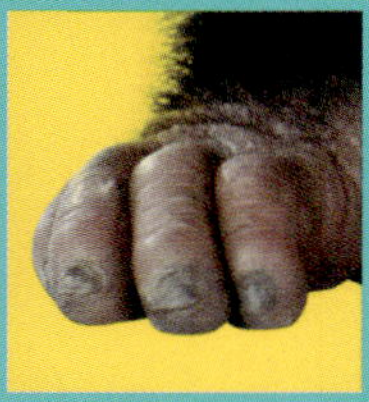

toes

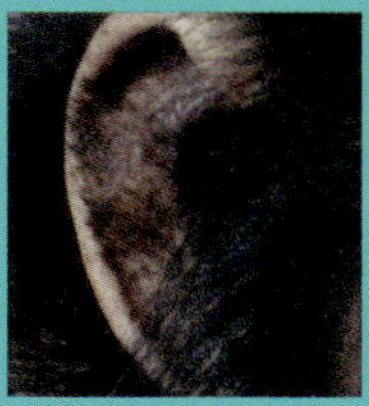

an ear

a mouth

Silverback gorilla

Fully grown male gorillas are often called silverbacks due to the silvery fur that develops as they get older. The most dominant silverback will lead the troop, or group, of apes.

Silver-colored fur

Strong arms

How do chimpanzees use tools?

Howling monkeys

The howler monkey's call is louder than an ambulance siren and can be heard from up to 3 miles (5 km) away! A male monkey will howl to claim an area as its territory.

Howler monkeys are among the loudest animals on Earth!

Learning language

Like chimps, other apes are also very clever. An orangutan named Chantek was raised by humans and taught sign language. Chantek learned over 150 signs and could understand spoken English. He even learned to use his "allowance" to buy his favorite treats!

Primates have forward-facing eyes like humans.

BIG BEARS

Polar bears are the biggest carnivores (meat eaters) on land. They feed mainly on seals but also eat walruses and beluga whales. They hunt on the pack ice in the cold Arctic sea, but rising global temperatures are melting the ice where they live. Some hungry polar bears have even visited nearby human settlements to look for food.

Polar bear

Grizzly bear

This bear's name comes from their fur, which is often tipped with white, giving them a "grizzled" look. Grizzly bears are omnivores. They eat both meat and plants, including fish, rodents, moose, leaves, and nuts.

Cozy caves and hollow trees

Bears find safe places where they can sleep through cold weather in winter. They sleep deeply in their dens but can wake up quickly if needed. Mother bears give birth in the den. When springtime comes, the cubs have grown and are ready to explore.

Brown bear mother and cub

What do polar bears like to eat?

Panda power

The giant panda may look cuddly, but they can be dangerous to humans. They live alone and spend 12 hours a day eating, mainly bamboo!

Can you point to?

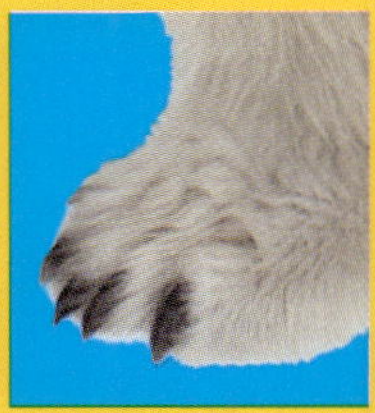

claws

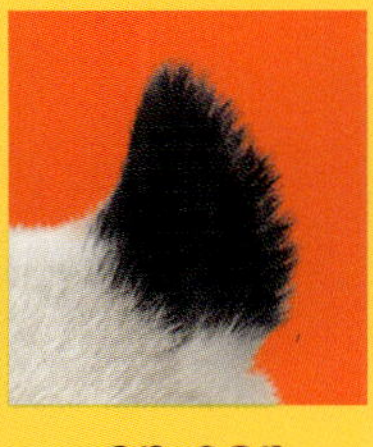

an ear

a snout

SUPER SENSES

We have five senses: sight, hearing, touch, taste and smell. Some animals, such as dolphins, bats, and toothed whales, use an extra sense called echolocation. They make clicking noises and listen to the echos that bounce back. Louder, longer echos can mean a large object. This helps them to "see" in dark or murky conditions and hunt for food.

Dolphins have no sense of smell!

Bottlenose dolphin

Cone-shaped teeth

A dog's noseprint is unique, like a human's fingerprint.

Smelling the air

A dog's sense of smell is 40 times better than a human's. Dogs, like this German shepherd, are used in search and rescue missions because they can sniff out lost or missing people.

Spiders taste and smell using their legs!

How does a dolphin find its way in murky water?

Eyes can see clearly underwater.

Taste and feel

Spiders use the hairs that cover their bodies to help them "hear." Their hairs sense vibrations, and are so sensitive that a spider can tell the difference between a fly and a bee caught in its web.

The feathers around an owl's face focus sounds, like our ears do.

Seeing in the dark

The barn owl's large eyes help it to see its prey clearly in the dark. Owls' eyes are fixed in their sockets, so they have to rotate their whole head to look around. They can see the smallest movements and hear the quietest sounds.

PARENTS AND BABIES

Insects have the most babies. The queen African driver ant can lay up to 3 to 4 million eggs every 25 days! Some animals, such as baby fish, can look after themselves as soon as they are born. Other animal babies, such as female elephants, stay with their mothers their whole lives.

Clownfish

Carry me!

Some female mammals carry their young in a pouch until they are fully developed. They are known as marsupials. Koalas and kangaroos are marsupials.

Race to the sea

Mother turtles lay their eggs in nests on land, and then return to the ocean. When their babies hatch, they must get to the sea before they are spotted by predators such as birds and crabs.

White bands develop from front to back after the clownfish is born.

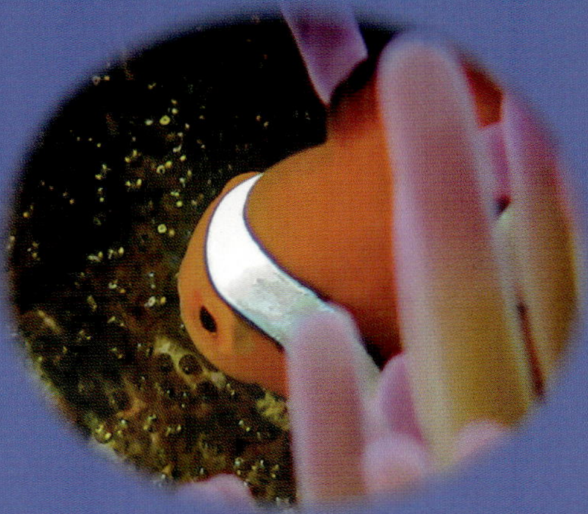

Fan club

After the female clownfish has laid her eggs, the male clownfish protects them until they hatch. He fans the eggs with his fins.

Where do clownfish live?

Can you point to?

a nose

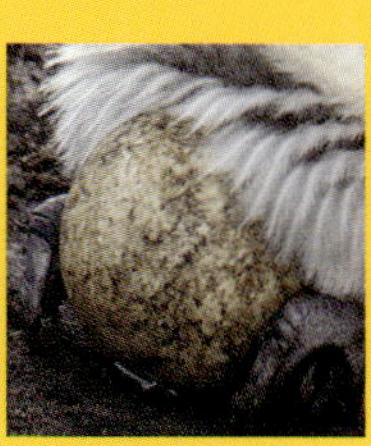

an egg

a stripy tail

Stay-at-home dads

Penguin parents take turns to look after their young. A penguin dad keeps the egg warm all through the winter while the mother penguin goes to the ocean in search of food to bring back to the newly hatched chick.

LONGEST JOURNEYS

The Arctic tern makes the longest journey of any animal. It migrates to find food and warmer weather, flying from the top of the Earth to the bottom and back again in one year. That's a very long way for a little bird to fly!

Arctic tern migration

Monarch butterfly

These butterflies migrate each year from as far north as Canada to the warmer weather of Mexico in the south. That's around 2,485 miles (4,000 km)!

Monarch butterflies

Weighs only 0.22 pound (100 g)

What is migration?

When animals make a long journey to find food or to breed (have babies) this is called migration. Many animals, including fish, turtles, deer, dragonflies, and butterflies, migrate each year.

Arctic terns may travel more than 43,500 miles (70,000 km) in a year.

Across the oceans

The gray whale makes a yearly migration. From the warm waters off the coast of Mexico where its young are born, it travels north to feed in the cooler waters of the Arctic.

Gray whales make a round trip of 12,427 miles (20,000 km) each year!

Why do Arctic terns fly so far?

Arctic tern

Smooth, black head

Arctic terns dive down to catch fish as they travel.

Adélie penguins

These penguins live in the Antarctic—the coldest place on Earth. Each year, they make a 8,000-mile (13,000-km) trip from their feeding grounds to their breeding grounds and back again!

BEST BUILDERS

Some animals live out in the open, but others like to build their own safe place to live. Termites build mounds for their colony to live in. There are tunnels and chimneys to allow air to flow through. This enormous termite mound is taller than a giraffe—an incredible feat for animals that are only 0.5 inch (12 mm) long!

Bee honeycomb

Worker bees make their nest from wax. They build six-sided (hexagonal) cells or pockets to store nectar, pollen, and honey. The queen bee lays her eggs in these too. The honeycomb is very light but strong.

This bee nest hangs from a tree branch.

Termite mound

The mound is made from soil, saliva, and droppings!

Millions of termites live in the nest inside the base of the mound.

Termite worker

Beaver's lodge

Beavers' homes are called lodges. They cut down trees with their teeth and use the branches to dam a stream. This creates a pond. The beavers then make an island out of more branches and stones in the middle of the pond, and build the lodge on top!

Weaver's nest

Male weaver birds are incredible nest-builders and are the only known bird that is able to tie knots. They use this skill to build nests made of twigs, leaves, and grass. The female will inspect the nest before she decides to live there.

An adult giraffe can be up to almost 20 feet (6 m) tall. Some termite mounds can be 30 feet (9 m) tall.

FAST FLYERS

The peregrine falcon is the world's fastest animal. It can reach speeds of up to 242 miles (390 km) per hour when diving to catch its prey! Like a jet plane, it has a smooth body shape that is built for speed.

Long wingspan

Peregrine falcon

Tail feathers help with turning.

Hummingbirds

Hummingbirds beats their wings so fast that they make a humming sound. They beat around 80 times every second! It is the only bird that can fly like a helicopter: up, down, sideways, forward, and backward!

A long beak sucks up nectar.

Hummingbirds need to eat a lot of nectar to keep up their energy levels.

Gliding albatross

The albatross has the longest wingspan of any living bird. From tip to tip, the wings can measure almost 10 feet (3 m)! Albatrosses save energy by gliding on the wind. They can fly for hours without having to flap their wings.

Acrobatic swift

Swifts have special wings that are long and narrow to help them fly quickly and skilfully as they dart around chasing their food. They are the fastest birds in level flight.

Why does the peregrine falcon need a smooth body?

Can you point to?

talons

flowers

a wing tip

GLOSSARY

Camouflage – a pattern on an animal's fur, feathers, or skin that helps it to blend in with its surroundings.

Carnivore – a creature that mainly eats other animals.

Colony – a group of animals or plants of the same type living together.

Herbivore – a creature that mainly eats plants.

Mammal – an animal that breathes air, has a backbone, and grows hair or fur. Their babies are born alive and are fed by their mother's milk.

Markings – the patterns or different colors on an animal's skin, feathers or fur.

Marsupial – a type of mammal. The females have a pouch on their bellies where their babies live and feed when they are young.

Migration – when animals make a long journey to find food or to breed (have babies). Many animals, including fish, turtles, deer, dragonflies, and butterflies, migrate each year.

Omnivore – a creature that eats both plants and other animals.

Primate – an animal with hands with five fingers, flat fingernails, and forward-facing eyes. This animal group includes lemurs, bush babies, monkeys, apes, and humans.

Territory – the area that an animal defends as belonging to them or their group or family.

Venomous – being able to inject a substance (venom) by a bite or sting, for protection or to kill prey.

INDEX